Copyright

Gather Up Yo' Fine Clothes, originally published as *Fine Clothes to the Jew*, as well as the essays "The Negro Artist and the Racial Mountain" and "These Bad New Negroes: A Critique on Critics" are in the public domain.

Book Cover by Taylor Elyse Morrison, featuring the public domain image, "Langston Hughes as a student at Lincoln University, Pennsylvania", sourced from the New York Public Library Digital Collections.

Illustrations by Taylor Elyse Morrison

AF430313

Table of Contents

Preface
Written by Taylor Elyse Morrison

Gather Up Yo' Fine Clothes, originally titled *Fine Clothes to the Jew*, was quite the conversation starter when it first launched in 1927. Hughes' second published book proved to be a departure from *The Weary Blues*.

The original title made me squirm even as I read it at the tail end of 2022. It feels almost fated that this work would enter the public domain after the year we've had. A year when Kanye West threatened to go "death con 3" on Jewish people, Kyrie Irving tweeted a movie supporting extremist Black Hebrew Israelite ideology, and antisemitic incidents in the States are at an all-time high.

Fine Clothes to the Jew references a line in Hughes' poem, "Hard Luck." And the line in the poem references a colloquialism used by Black folks at the time. When you were low on money, you'd take your best clothes to the pawnshop. Many of these shops in Harlem were owned by Jewish families.

I think if we were to ask Hughes for his take on the title, he'd tell us the slang could certainly be considered indelicate—a term we'll hear him use in an upcoming essay—but not meant to be hateful.

Though that may not have been Hughes' intent, the phrase highlights the tension that has, and continues to, exist between Black and Jewish communities. Both groups have experienced centuries of global oppression, and members of both groups have perpetuated harm against each other in America.

The pawnshop offers an apt metaphor for this nuanced relationship. For poor Black folks in Harlem, pawning off their finest possessions was one of the only access points to capital in a racist society. And in the earlier 19th century, Harlem was home to over 175,000 Jewish people—the third largest population of Jews globally.

Though Jewish immigrants were initially barred from certain trades, they had enough proximity to whiteness to own property and run retail shops of their own. For some Jews, the journey of assimilation included assimilating into the exploitative practices that form the foundation of our country.

There are bright spots of solidarity in Black-Jewish relations throughout each chapter of America's history: Music made. Cases fought. Freedom rides ridden. There are also deep wells of distrust, misunderstanding, harm, and a desire for each group's oppression to be acknowledged rather than overlooked or one-upped. When each community focuses on tearing the other down, we're too distracted to tear down the system itself.

Hughes understood that truth. He wrote in his autobiography that he was the descendant of a Jewish slave trader, and he didn't shy away from talking about both Black and Jewish struggles. Perhaps his complex personal heritage made the parallels between both groups even more apparent. As Hughes later asserted in his *Chicago Defender* essays: fascism was fascism, whether it was in Nazi Germany or the Jim Crow South. Always unacceptable, and Hughes believed it was in their shared interest to push back against it together.

Ultimately, the original title has almost nothing to do with this collection of poems. We're left to wonder why Hughes made the, in his words, "unfortunate choice" to highlight that particular line. There were critics in his day who found it to be both ineffective and tangential, but that title was not the marquis point of controversy. Though relatively well-received by white critics, the book's portrayal of Black folks concerned many Black critics.

Hughes' inclusion of all kinds of Black people: prostitutes and drinkers and poor folks and gamblers, went against the respectable image that contemporaries like W. E. B. Du Bois wanted to project.

The discourse around respectability politics and representation is as old as the Black community in America. Back then, peers accused Hughes of playing into stereotypes by showcasing, with brutal honesty, Black narratives beyond the Talented Tenth. Today, we talk about how Black actors seem to pander to mostly white Oscar voters when they star in a film that centers on racial trauma. Hughes makes his position abundantly clear in *Fine Clothes*: everyday people deserve to have their stories told just as much as the elite do. We're not obligated to center whiteness or to sugarcoat reality to create something excellent.

And create something excellent he did. Hughes' biographer, Arnold Rampersad, called the collection "by far Hughes' greatest collection of verse."

Since its publication nearly a century ago, *Fine Clothes* has sparked conversations both among the Harlem Renaissance's literati and literary scholars alike, but that conversation hasn't included the everyday reader—until now.

Though I've made the decision to change the title from *Fine Clothes to the Jew* to *Gather Up Yo' Fine Clothes* for this reprint, I believe the legacy of Hughes' initial, indelicate title choice still serves a purpose today. Each poem invites us to talk, to listen, and to question who we're centering in our conversations—

across class, gender, culture, skin tone, and creed. May those conversations lead us towards increased empathy and solidarity.

The new title, also a line from "Hard Times," captures both the joy and the hardships Hughes explores in his poetry. One could just as easily gather up their fine clothes for a night of dancing as for church or a trip to the pawnshop.

This reprint, the first standalone reprint since 1927, is prefaced by two of Hughes' essays, "The Negro Artist and the Racial Mountain" and "These Bad New Negroes: A Critique on Critics."

These essays showcase the contemporary criticism Hughes received and his direct responses, laying the foundation for you to engage with this poetic work and form opinions of your own.

THE NEGRO ARTIST
AND THE RACIAL MOUNTAIN

The Negro Artist and the Racial Mountain

Originally Published in The Nation in June 1926

One of the most promising of the young Negro poets said to me once, "I want to be a poet—not a Negro poet," meaning, I believe, "I want to write like a white poet"; meaning subconsciously, "I would like to be a white poet"; meaning behind that, "I would like to be white." And I was sorry the young man said that, for no great poet has ever been afraid of being himself. And I doubted then that, with his desire to run away spiritually from his race, this boy would ever be a great poet. But this is the mountain standing in the way of any true Negro art in America—this urge within the race toward whiteness, the desire to pour racial individuality into the mold of American standardization, and to be as little Negro and as much American as possible.

But let us look at the immediate background of this young poet. His family is of what I suppose one would call the Negro middle class: people who are by no means rich yet never uncomfortable nor hungry—smug, contented, respectable folk, members of the Baptist church. The father goes to work every morning. He is a chief steward at a large white club. The mother sometimes does fancy sewing or supervises parties for the rich families of the town. The children go to a mixed school. In the home they read white papers and magazines. And the mother often says, "Don't be like niggers" when the children are bad. A frequent phrase from the father is, "Look how well a white man does things." And so the word white comes to be unconsciously a symbol of all virtues. It holds for the children beauty, morality, and money. The whisper of "I want to be white" runs silently through their minds. This young poet's home is, I believe, a fairly typical home of the colored middle class. One sees immediately how difficult it would be for an artist born in such a home to interest himself in interpreting the beauty of his own people. He is never taught to see that beauty. He is taught rather not to see it, or if he does, to be ashamed of it when it is not according to Caucasian patterns.

For racial culture the home of a self-styled "high-class" Negro has nothing better to offer. Instead there will perhaps be more aping of things white than in a less cultured or less wealthy home. The father is perhaps a doctor, lawyer, land-owner, or politician. The mother may be a social worker, or a teacher, or she may do nothing and have a maid. Father is often dark but he has usually married the lightest woman he could find. The family attend a fashionable church where few really colored faces are to be found. And they themselves draw a color line. In the North they go to white theaters and white movies. And in the South they have at least two cars and house "like white folks." Nordic manners, Nordic faces, Nordic hair, Nordic art (if any), and an Episcopal heaven. A very high mountain indeed for the would-be racial artist to climb in order to discover himself and his people.

But then there are the low-down folks, the so-called common element, and they are the majority—may the Lord be praised! The people who have their nip of gin on Saturday nights and are not too important to themselves or the community, or too well fed, or too learned to watch the lazy world go round. They live on Seventh Street in Washington or State Street in Chicago and they do not particularly care whether they are like white folks or anybody else. Their joy runs, bang! into ecstasy. Their religion soars to a shout. Work maybe a little today, rest a little tomorrow. Play awhile. Sing awhile. O, let's dance! These common people are not afraid of spirituals, as for a long time their more intellectual brethren were, and jazz is their child. They furnish a wealth of colorful, distinc-tive material for any artist because they still hold their own individuality in the face of American standardizations. And perhaps these common people will give to the world its truly great Negro artist, the one who is not afraid to be himself. Whereas the better-class Negro would tell the artist what to do, the people at least let him alone when he does appear. And they are not ashamed of him—if they know he exists at all. And they accept what beauty is their own without question.

Certainly there is, for the American Negro artist who can escape the restrictions the more advanced among his own group would put upon him, a great field of unused material ready for his art. Without going outside his race, and even among the better classes with their "white" culture and conscious American manners, but still Negro enough to be different, there is sufficient matter to furnish a black artist with a lifetime of creative work. And when he chooses to touch on the relations between Negroes and whites in this country, with their innumerable overtones and undertones, surely, and especially for literature and the drama, there is an inexhaustible supply of themes at hand. To these the Negro artist can give his racial individuality, his heritage of rhythm and warmth, and his incongruous humor that so often, as in the Blues, becomes ironic laughter mixed with tears. But let us look again at the mountain.

A prominent Negro clubwoman in Philadelphia paid eleven dollars to hear Raquel Meller sing Andalusian popular songs. But she told me a few weeks before she would not think of going to hear "that woman," Clara Smith, a great black artist, sing Negro folksongs. And many an upper-class Negro church, even now, would not dream of employing a spiritual in its services. The drab melodies in white folks' hymnbooks are much to be preferred. "We want to worship the Lord correctly and quietly. We don't believe in 'shouting.' Let's be dull like the Nordics," they say, in effect.

The road for the serious black artist, then, who would produce a racial art is most certainly rocky and the mountain is high. Until recently he received almost no encouragement for his work from either white or colored people. The fine novels of Chesnutt go out of print with neither race noticing their passing. The quaint charm and humor of Dunbar's dialect verse brought to him, in his day, largely the same kind of encouragement one would give a sideshow freak (A colored man writing poetry! How odd!) or a clown (How amusing!).

The present vogue in things Negro, although it may do as much harm as good for the budding colored artist, has at least done this: it has brought him forcibly to the attention of his own people among whom for so long, unless the other race had noticed him beforehand, he was a prophet with little honor. I understand that Charles Gilpin acted for years in Negro theaters without any special acclaim from his own, but when Broadway gave him eight curtain calls, Negroes, too, began to beat a tin pan in his honor. I know a young colored writer, a manual worker by day, who had been writing well for the colored magazines for some years, but it was not until he recently broke into the white publications and his first book was accepted by a prominent New York publisher that the "best" Negroes in his city took the trouble to discover that he lived there. Then almost immediately they decided to give a grand dinner for him. But the society ladies were careful to whisper to his mother that perhaps she'd better not come. They were not sure she would have an evening gown.

The Negro artist works against an undertow of sharp criticism and misunderstanding from his own group and unintentional bribes from the whites. "O, be respectable, write about nice people, show how good we are," say the Negroes.

"Be stereotyped, don't go too far, don't shatter our illusions about you, don't amuse us too seriously. We will pay you," say the whites. Both would have told Jean Toomer not to write "Cane." The colored people did not praise it. The white people did not buy it. Most of the colored people who did read "Cane" hate it. They are afraid of it. Although the critics gave it good reviews the public remained indifferent. Yet (excepting the work of Du Bois) "Cane" contains the finest prose written by a Negro in America. And like the singing of Robeson, it is truly racial.

But in spite of the Nordicized Negro intelligentsia and the desires of some white editors we have an honest American Negro literature already with us. Now I await the rise of the Negro theater. Our folk music, having achieved world-wide fame, offers itself to the genius of the great individual American Negro composer who is to come. And within the next decade I expect to see the work of a growing school of colored artists who paint and model the beauty of dark faces and create with new technique the expressions of their own soul-world. And the Negro dancers who will dance like flame and the singers who will continue to carry our songs to all who listen—they will be with us in even greater numbers tomorrow.

Most of my own poems are racial in theme and treatment, derived from the life I know. In many of them I try to grasp and hold some of the meanings and rhythms of jazz. I am as sincere as I know how to be in these poems and yet after every reading I answer questions like these from my own people: Do you think Negroes should always write about Negroes? I wish you wouldn't read some of your poems to white folks. How do you find anything interesting in a place like a cabaret? Why do you write about black people? You aren't black. What makes you do so many jazz poems?

But jazz to me is one of the inherent expressions of Negro life in America: the eternal tom-tom beating in the Negro soul—the tom-tom of revolt against weariness in a white world, a world of subway trains, and work, work, work; the tom-tom of joy and laughter, and pain swallowed in a smile. Yet the Philadelphia clubwoman is ashamed to say that her race created it and she does not like me to write about it. The old subconscious "white is best" runs through her mind. Years of study under white teachers, a lifetime of white books, pictures, and papers, and white manners, morals, and Puritan standards made her dislike the spirituals. And now she turns up her nose at jazz and all its manifestations—likewise almost everything else distinctly racial. She doesn't care for the Winold Reiss portraits of Negroes because they are "too Negro." She does not want a true picture of herself from anybody. She wants the artist to flatter her, to make the white world believe that all Negroes are as smug and as near white in soul as she wants to be. But, to my mind, it is the duty of the younger Negro artist, if he accepts any duties at all from outsiders, to change through the force of his art that old whispering "I want to be white," hidden in the aspirations of his people, to "Why should I want to be white? I am a Negro—and beautiful"?

So I am ashamed for the black poet who says, "I want to be a poet, not a Negro poet," as though his own racial world were not as interesting as any other world. I am ashamed, too, for the colored artist who runs from the painting of Negro faces to the painting of sunsets after the manner of the academicians because he fears the strange un-whiteness of his own features. An artist must be free to choose what he does, certainly, but he must also never be afraid to do what he might choose.

Let the blare of Negro jazz bands and the bellowing voice of

Bessie Smith singing the Blues penetrate the closed ears of the colored near-intellectuals until they listen and perhaps understand. Let Paul Robeson singing Water Boy, and Rudolph Fisher writing about the streets of Harlem, and Jean Toomer holding the heart of Georgia in his hands, and Aaron Douglas drawing strange black fantasies cause the smug Negro middle class to turn from their white, respectable, ordinary books and papers to catch a glimmer of their own beauty. We younger Negro artists who create now intend to express our individual dark-skinned selves without fear or shame. If white people are pleased we are glad. If they are not, it doesn't matter. We know we are beautiful. And ugly too. The tom-tom cries and the tom-tom laughs. If colored people are pleased we are glad. If they are not, their displeasure doesn't matter either. We build our temples for tomorrow, strong as we know how, and we stand on top of the mountain, free within ourselves.

THESE
BAD
NEW
NEG
ROES
:
A critique
on critics

These Bad New Negroes: A Critique on Critics
Originally published in the Pittsburgh Courier in April 1927

Tired of living penniless on bread and figs in Genoa, I found myself a job on a ship bound for New York in the fall, 1924. When, after many days of scrubbing decks on my part, the boat reached Manhattan. There was a letter waiting for me from my mother saying, "We're living in Washington now. Come home." And I went.

I'd never been in Washington before but I found it a city as beautiful as Paris and full of nice colored people, many of them nice looking and living in nice houses. For my mother and me, the city was a sort of ancestral shrine of which I had heard much. The great John M. Langston, senator, educator, and grand-uncle of mine had once lived there. Indeed, I was to stop with descendants of his and, of course, I would meet the best people. And I did.

But since this is to be an article on literature and art, I must get on into the subject. For two years, working at sea and travelling, I had been away from books. Many of my own I had thrown into the ocean because I found life more attractive than the printed word. But now I wanted to read again and talk about literature so I set out to borrow, in good Negro fashion, a copy of Jean Toomer's *Cane*. "What!" said the well-bred Washington folk. "*Cane?*" they repeated, not many having heard of it. Then I was soon given to understand by the female heads of several nice families that *Cane* was a vulgar book and that no one read it. "Why do you young folks write that way?" they asked. I offered no protest for I had not heard the question before and I am not much at answering questions quickly. But, amazed, I thought how a prophet is without honor in his own country, since Jean Toomer was born and had lived in Washington. *Cane* had received critical recognition all over America, and even in Europe, as a beautiful book, yet in the society of the author's own home town it was almost unknown. And those who knew it thought it something low and indecent. Whenever *Cane* was mentioned the best Washingtonians posted this question: "Why doesn't Jean Toomer write about nice people?" And I began to think they wanted to add, "Like ourselves."

When Rudolph Fisher's *City of Refuge* appeared in the *Atlantic Monthly* (Washington is Fisher's home-town, too) the best persons again asked the same thing: "Why can't you young folks write about nice people? Rudolph Fisher knows decent folks." And then I knew the "nice people" meant themselves.

Then Alain Locke's *New Negro* appeared on the scene with stories by Toomer, Fisher, Eric Walrond, Zora Hurston, Matheus, and none of them were nice stories in the Washington sense of the word. "Too bad," they said. But the storm broke on the Reiss drawings. They were terrible! And anyone defending them had to answer questions like these: "Why does he make his subjects so colored?" (As though they weren't colored.) And of the two school teachers pictured in the book: "Couldn't he find any better looking school teachers to paint than these two women?" (As though all teachers should resemble the high-yellow ladies dominating the Washington school system.) And always: "Does he call this art?" I said it was art and that the dark-skinned school teachers were beautiful. But one day a nice old grandmother, with whom I disliked to disagree, summed up everybody's aversion to Fisher, Tomer, Walrond, and the Reiss drawings in one indefinite but pregnant remark, "Lord help these bad New Negroes!"

Now that there has appeared in the colored press a definite but rather uncritical aversion to much of the work of the younger Negro writers and particularly myself; and because the Negro press reflects to a certain extent the minds of its readers, it is time to attempt to uncover the reasons for this dislike toward the "New Negro." I present these as possible solutions:

1. The best Negroes, including the newspaper critics, still think white people are better than colored people. It follows, in their minds, that since the drawings of Negroes do not look like the drawings of white people they are bad art.
2. The best Negroes believe that what white people think about Negroes is more important than what Negroes think about themselves. Then it follows that because a story by Zora Hurston does not tend to make white people think all Negroes good, then said story by Zora Hurston is a bad story.
3. Many of the so-called best Negroes are in a sort of *nouveau riche* class, so from the snobbishness of their positions they hold the false belief that if the stories of Fisher were only about better class people they would be better stories.
4. Again, many of the best Negroes, including the newspaper critics, are not really cultured Negroes after all and, therefore, have little appreciation of any art and no background from which to view either their own or the white man's books or pictures.

Perhaps none of these reasons are true reasons but I offer them for consideration. Now I shall proceed to the defense.

Art is a reflection of life or an individual's comment on life. No one has labeled the work of the better known younger Negro writers as untrue to life. It may be largely about humble people, but three-fourths of the Negroes are humble people. Yet I understand these "best" colored folks when

they say that little has been written about them. I am sorry
and I wish some one would put them into a nice story or
a nice novel. But I fear for them if ever a really powerful
work is done about their lives. Such a story would show not
only their excellencies but their pseudo-culture as well, their
slavish devotion to Nordic standards, their snobbishness,
their detachment from the Negro masses, and their vast sense
of importance to themselves. A book like that from a Negro
writer, even though true and beautiful, would be more thor-
oughly disliked than the stories of low-class Negroes now
being written. And it would be more wrathfully damned than
Nigger Heaven, at present vibrating throughout the land in its
eleventh edition.

It seems to me too bad that the discussions of Mr. Van
Vechten's novel in the colored press finally became hysteri-
cal and absurd. No book could possibly be as bad as *Nigger
Heaven* has been painted. And no book has ever been better
advertised by those who wished to damn it. Because it was
declared obscene everybody wanted to read it and I'll venture
to say that more Negroes bought it than ever purchased a
book by a Negro author. Which is all very fine because *Nigger
Heaven* is not a bad book. It will do nice people good to
read it and maybe it will broaden their minds a bit. Certainly
the book is true to the life it pictures. There are cabarets in
Harlem and both white and colored people who are nation-
ally known and respected can be found almost any night at
Small's. I've seen ministers there—nobody considers caba-
ret-going indecent any longer. And college boys, as you know,
do have affairs with loose women. Some even given allowanc-
es and put through medical school by such generous females.
But nowhere in the novel does the author represent his
college boy as a typical Negro college boy. And nowhere does
he say he is writing about the whole Negro race. I admit I am
ill-mannered onslaught against Mr. Van Vechten. The sincere,

friendly, and helpful interest in things Negro of this sophisticated author, as shown in his published reviews and magazine articles, should at least have commanded serious, rather than vulgar, reviews of his book.

That many of the Negro write-ups of my own new collection of poems, *Fine Clothes to the Jew*, were unfavorable was not surprising to me. And to be charged with painting the whole Negro race in my poems did not amaze me either. Colored critics are given to accusing all works of art touching on the Negro of portraying and representing *all* Negro life. *Porgy*, about a beggar in Charleston, is said by them to picture all Negroes as beggars, yet nowhere does DuBose Heyward imply such a thing. Newspaper critics, of course, came to the same amazing conclusion about *Nigger Heaven* picturing all Negroes as cabaret goers. And now *Fine Clothes to the Jew* "low-rates" everybody of color, in their opinion.

In analyzing their reviews of my book their main objections against my work seem to be based on the reasons I am listing with my own comments following:

1. White people will gain a bad impression of Negroes from my poems. This then implies that a Negro artist should create largely for the benefit of and for the approval of white people. In answering this I ask these questions: Does George Bernard Shaw write his plays to show Englishmen how good the Irish are? Do any of the great Russian writers write novels for the purpose of showing the perfections of the Russians? Does any true artist anywhere work for the sake of what a limited group of people will think rather than for the sake of what he himself loves and wishes to interpret? It seems to me that there are plenty of propagandists for the Negro, but too few art-ists, too few poets, too few interpreters and re-

1. cords of racial life, whether choosing their material from the masses or from the best people.
2. My poems are indelicate. But so is life.
3. I write about "harlots and gin-bibers." But they are human. Solomon, Homer, Shakespeare, and Walt Whitman were not afraid or ashamed to include them.
4. "Red Silk Stockings." An ironical poem deploring the fact that in certain southern rural communities there is little work for a beautiful colored girl to do other than the selling of her body—a fact for one to weep over rather than disdain to recognize.
5. I do not write in the conventional forms of Keats, Poe, Dunbar or McKay. But I do not write chiefly because I'm interested in forms—in making a sonnet or a rondeau. I write because I want to say what I have to say. And I choose the form which seems to me best to express my thoughts. I fail to see why I should be expected to copy someone else's modes of expression when it amuses me to attempt to create forms of my own. Certainly the Shakespearean sonnet would be no mould in which to express the life of Beale Street or Lenox Avenue. Nor could the emotions of State Street be captured in rondeau. I am not interested in doing tricks with rhymes. I am interested in reproducing the human soul, if I can.
6. I am prostituting my talent. But even the income from a very successful book of poems is not worth the prostitution of one's talent. I make much more money as a bell-hop than as a poet.
7. I deal with low life. But I ask this: Is life among the better classes any cleaner or any more worthy of a poet's consideration?
8. Blues are not poetry. Those who have made a more thorough study of Negro folk verse than I, and who are authorities in this field, say that many Blues are excellent poetry. I refer to James Weldon Johnson, Dorothy Scar-

8. borough, Carl Van Vechten and H. O. Osgood in their
    published writings.
9. I am "supposed to be representative of Negro progress
    in the literary arts." To which I can only answer that I do
    not pretend, or ask anyone to suppose, that I officially
    represent anybody or anything other than myself. My po-
    ems are my own personal comments on life and represent
    me alone. I claim nothing more for them.

If the colored newspaper critics (excepting Dewey Jones and
Alice Dunbar Nelson) choose to read only the words I write
and not their meaning, if they choose to see only what they
call the ugliness of my verse and not the protest against ug-
liness which my poems contain, what can I do? Such obtuse
critics existed in the days of Wordsworth, Shelley, Burns, and
Dunbar—great poets with whose work I dare not compare
my own. Burns was maligned because he did not write of
Scottish nobles. And as Miss Nannie Burroughs says: "to
come down to the nasty now," Jean Toomer is without honor
in Washington. But certainly my life has been enlivened by the
gentle critics who called me a "gutter-rat" and "sewer-dwell-
er" right out in print! Variety—even in the weekly press, is the
spice of criticism.

Since I am said to be the "baddest" of the bad New Negroes,
I may as well express my own humble opinion on my young
contemporaries, although I may vary with the race newspa-
pers and the best Negroes. To me the stories of Rudolph
Fisher are beautiful although he deals with common folks.
To me it seems absurd to say that they are not elevating to
the race. The stories of Sherwood Anderson deal largely with
people of the same classes but white America calls him one
of the greatest of the moderns. If Rudolph Fisher can write
beautifully about a poor Negro migrant from the South, more
power to him. A well-written story, no matter what its subject,

is a contribution to the art of the Negro and I am amazed at
the educated prudes who say it isn't. Jean Toomer is an artist
to be proud of. Wallace Thurman, Countee Cullen with his
marvelous command of technique and his poems of passion
and free love, Zora Hurston with her fine handling of Negro
dialect, Edward Silvera and the newer poets, all are contrib-
uting something worthwhile to the literature of the race. To
me it seems that we have much to be proud of in the work of
these younger colored writers whom the lady in Washington
so disapprovingly called the "bad New Negroes."

A NOTE
ON BLUES

A Note on Blues

The first eight and the last nine poems in this book are writ-
ten after the manner of the Negro folk-songs known as *Blues*.
The *Blues*, unlike the *Spirituals*, have a strict poetic pattern: one
long line repeated and a third line to rhyme with the first two.
Sometimes the second line in repetition is slightly changed
and sometimes, but very seldom, it is omitted. The mood of
the *Blues* is almost always despondency, but when they are
sung people laugh.

BLUES

Hey!

Sun's a settin',
This is what I'm gonna sing.
Sun's a settin',
This is what I'm gonna sing:
I feels de blues a comin',
Wonder what de blues'll bring?

Hard Luck

When hard luck overtakes you
Nothin' for you to do.
When hard luck overtakes you
Nothin' for you to do.
Gather up yo' fine clothes
An' sell 'em to de Jew.

Jew takes yo' fine clothes,
Gives you a dollar an' a half.
Jew takes yo' fine clothes,
Gives you a dollar an' a half.
Go to de bootleg's,
Git some gin to make you laugh.

If I was a mule I'd
Git me a waggon to haul.
If I was a mule I'd
Git a waggon to haul.
I'm so low-down I
Ain't even got a stall.

Misery

Play de blues for me.
Play de blues for me.
No other music
'Ll ease ma misery.

Sing a soothin' song.
Said a soothin' song,
Cause de man I love's done
Done me wrong.

Can't you understand,
O, understand
A good woman's cryin'
For a no-good man?

Black gal like me,
Black gal like me
'S got to hear a blues
For her misery.

Suicide

Ma sweet good man has
Packed his trunk and left.
Ma sweet good man has
Packed his trunk and left.
Nobody to love me:
I'm gonna kill ma self.

I'm gonna buy me a knife with
A blade ten inches long.
Gonna buy me a knife with
A blade ten inches long.
Shall I carve ma self or
That man that done me wrong?

'Lieve I'll jump in de river
Eighty-nine feet deep.
'Lieve I'll jump in de river
Eighty-nine feet deep.
Cause de river's quiet
An' a po', po' gal can sleep.

Bad Man

I'm a bad, bad man
Cause everybody tells me so.
I'm a bad, bad man.
Everybody tells me so.
I takes ma meanness and ma licker
Everwhere I go.

I beats ma wife an'
I beats ma side gal too.
Beats ma wife an'
Beats ma side gal too.
Don't know why I do it but
It keeps me from feelin' blue.

I'm so bad I
Don't even want to be good.
So bad, bad, bad I
Don't even want to be good.
I'm goin' to de devil an'
I wouldn't go to heaben if I could.

Gypsy Man

Ma man's a gypsy
Cause he never does come home.
Ma man's a gypsy,—
He never does come home.
I'm gonna be a gypsy woman
Fer I can't stay here alone.

Once I was in Memphis,
I mean Tennessee.
Once I was in Memphis,
Said Tennessee.
But I had to leave cause
Nobody there was good to me.

I met a yellow papa,
He took ma last thin dime.
Met a yellow papa,
He took ma last thin dime.
I give it to him cause I loved him
But I'll have mo' sense next time.

Love, Oh, love is
Such a strange disease.
Love, Oh, love is
Such a strange disease.
When it hurts yo' heart you
Sho can't find no ease.

Po' Boy Blues

When I was home de
Sunshine seemed like gold.
When I was home de
Sunshine seemed like gold.
Since I come up North de
Whole damn world's turned cold.

I was a good boy,
Never done no wrong.
Yes, I was a good boy,
Never done no wrong,
But this world is weary
An' de road is hard an' long.

I fell in love with
A gal I thought was kind.
Fell in love with
A gal I thought was kind.
She made me lose ma money
An' almost lose ma mind.

Weary, weary,
Weary early in de morn.
Weary, weary,
Early, early in de morn.
I's so weary
I wish I'd never been born.

Homesick Blues

De railroad bridge's
A sad song in de air.
De railroad bridge's
A sad song in de air.
Ever time de trains pass
I wants to go somewhere.

I went down to de station.
Ma heart was in ma mouth.
Went down to de station.
Heart was in ma mouth.
Lookin' for a box car
To roll me to de South.

Homesick blues, Lawd,
'S a terrible thing to have.
Homesick blues is
A terrible thing to have.
To keep from cryin'
I opens ma mouth an' laughs.

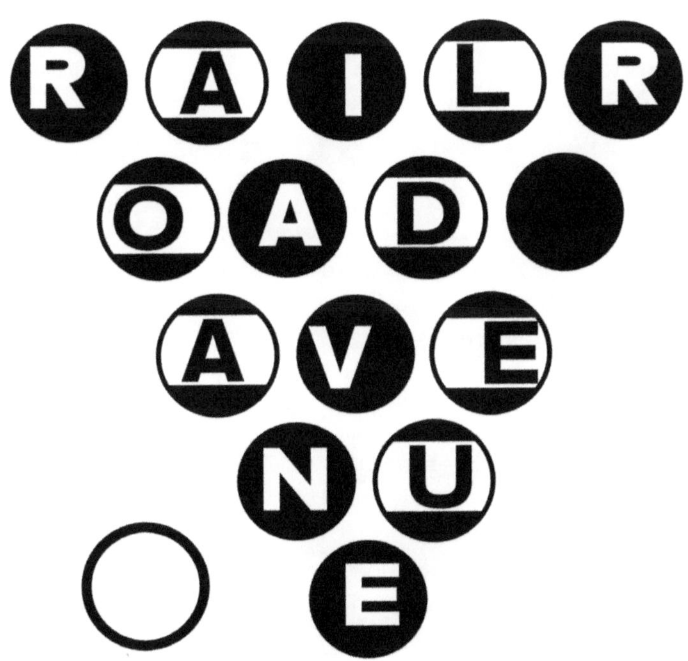
R A I L R
O A D
A V E
N U
E

Railroad Avenue

Dusk dark
On Railroad Avenue.
Lights in the fish joints,
Lights in the pool rooms.
A box-car some train
Has forgotten
In the middle of the
Block.
A player piano,
A victrola
        942
        Was the number.
A boy
Lounging on a corner.
A passing girl
With purple powdered skin.
        Laughter
        Suddenly
        Like a taut drum.
        Laughter
        Suddenly
        Neither truth nor lie.
        Laughter
Hardening the dusk dark evening.
        Laughter
Shaking the lights in the fish joints,
Rolling white balls in the pool rooms,
And leaving untouched the box-car
Some train has forgotten.

Brass Spitoons

Clean the spitoons, boy.
        Detroit,
        Chicago,
        Atlantic City,
        Palm Beach.
Clean the spitoons.
The steam in hotel kitchens,
And the smoke in hotel lobbies,
And the slime in hotel spitoons:
Part of my life.
        Hey, boy!
        A nickel,
        A dime,
        A dollar,
Two dollars a day.
        Hey, boy!
        A nickel,
        A dime,
        A dollar,
        Two dollars
Buys shoes for the baby.
House rent to pay.
Gin on Saturday,
Church on Sunday.
        My God!
Babies and gin and church
and women and Sunday
all mixed up with dimes and
dollars and clean spitoons
and house rent to pay.
        Hey, boy!
A bright bowl of brass is beautiful to the Lord.
Bright polished brass like the cymbals

Of King David's dancers,
Like the wine cups of Solomon.
        Hey, boy!
A clean spitoon on the altar of the Lord.
A clean bright spitoon all newly polished,—
At least I can offer that.
        Com'mere, boy!

Ruby Brown

She was young and beautiful
And golden like the sunshine
That warmed her body.
And because she was colored
Mayville had no place to offer her,
Nor fuel for the clean flame of joy
That tried to burn within her soul.

One day,
Sitting on old Mrs. Latham's back porch
Polishing the silver,
She asked herself two questions
And they ran something like this:
What can a colored girl do
On the money from a white woman's kitchen?
And ain't there any joy in this town?

Now the streets down by the river
Know more about this pretty Ruby Brown,
And the sinister shuttered houses of the bottoms
Hold a yellow girl
Seeking an answer to her questions.
The good church folk do not mention
Her name any more.

But the white men,
Habitués of the high shuttered houses,
Pay more money to her now
Than they ever did before,
When she worked in their kitchens.

The New Cabaret Girl

That little yaller gal
Wid blue-green eyes:
If her daddy ain't white
Would be a surprise.

She don't drink gin
An' she don't like corn.
I asked her one night
Where she was born.

An' she say, Honey,
I don't know
Where I come from
Or where I go.

That crazy little yaller gal
Wid blue-green eyes:
If her daddy ain't 'fay
Would be a surprise.

An' there she sets a cryin'
In de cabaret
A lookin' all sad
When she ought to play.

My God, I says,
You can't live that way!
Babe, you can't
Live that way!

Closing Time

Starter!

> Her face is pale
> In the doorway light.
> Her lips blood red
> And her skin blue white.

Taxi!

> I'm tired.
Deep…River…
> O, God, please!

The river and the moon hold memories.

> Cornets play.
> Dancers whirl.
> Death, be kind

What was the cover charge, kid?

> To a little drowned girl.

Prize Fighter

Only dumb guys fight.
      If I wasn't dumb
      I wouldn't be fightin'.
      I could make six dollars a day
      On the docks
      And I'd save more than I do now.
Only dumb guys fight.

Crap Game

Lemme roll 'em, boy.
I got ma tail curled!
If a seven don't come
'Leven ain't far away.
An' if I craps,
Dark baby,
Trouble
Don't last all de time.
Hit 'em, bones!

Ballad of Gin Mary

Carried me to de court,
Judge was settin' there.
Looked all around me,
Didn't have a friend nowhere.

Judge Pierce he says, Mary.
Old Judge says, Mary Jane,
Ever time I mounts this bench
I sees yo' face again.

O, Lawd! O, Lawd!
O, Lawd . . . Lawdee!
Seems like bad licker,
Judge, won't let me be.

Old Judge says you's a drunkard.
Fact is you worries me.
Gwine give you eighteen months
So licker'll let you be.

Eighteen months in jail!
O, eighteen months locked in!
Won't be so bad in jail
But I'll miss ma gin.

O, please sir, Judge, have mercy!
Have mercy, please, on me!
Old hard-faced Judge says eighteen months
Till licker'll let you be.

Death of Do Dirty: A Rounder's Song

O, you can't find a buddy
Any old time
'Ll help you out
When you ain't got a dime.

He was a friend o' mine.

They called him Do Dirty
Cause he was black
An' had cut his gal
An' shot a man in de back.

Ma friend o' mine.

But when I was hungry,
Had nothin' to eat,
He bought me corn bread
An' a stew o' meat.

Good friend o' mine.

An' when de cops got me
An' put me in jail
If Dirty had de money
He'd go ma bail.

O, friend o' mine.

That night he got kilt
I was standin' in de street.
Somebody comes by
An' says yo' boy is gettin' beat.

Ma friend o' mine.

But when I got there
An' seen de ambulance
A guy was sayin'
He ain't got a chance.

Best friend o' mine.

An' de ones that kilt him,—
Damn their souls,—
I'm gonna fill 'em up full o'
Bullet holes.

Ma friend o' mine.

Elevator Boy

I got a job now
Runnin' an elevator
In the Dennison Hotel in Jersey.
Job ain't no good though.
No money around.
        Jobs are just chances
        Like everything else.
        Maybe a little luck now,
        Maybe not.
        Maybe a good job sometimes:
        Step out o' the barrel, boy.
Two new suits an'
A woman to sleep with.
        Maybe no luck for a long time.
        Only the elevators
        Goin' up an' down,
        Up an' down,
        Or somebody elses' shoes
        To shine,
        Or greasy pots in a dirty kitchen.
I been runnin' this
Elevator too long.
Guess I'll quit now.

Porter

I must say
Yes, sir,
To you all the time.
Yes, sir!
Yes, sir!
All my days
Climbing up a great big mountain
Of yes, sirs!

Rich old white man
Owns the world.
Gimme yo' shoes
To shine.

Yes, sir!

Sport

Life
For him
Must be
The shivering of
A great drum
Beaten with swift sticks
Then at the closing hour
The lights go out
And there is no music at all
And death becomes
An empty cabaret
And eternity an unblown saxophone
And yesterday
A glass of gin
Drunk long
Ago.

Saturday Night

Play it once.
O, play some more.
Charlie is a gambler
An' Sadie is a whore.
     A glass o' whiskey
     An' a glass o' gin:
     Strut, Mr. Charlie,
     Till de dawn comes in.
Pawn yo' gold watch
An' diamond ring.
Git a quart o' licker,
Let's shake dat thing!
     Skee-de-dad! De-dad!
     Doo-doo-doo!
     Won't be nothin' left
     When de worms git through
     An' you's a long time
     Dead
     When you is
     Dead, too.
So beat dat drum, boy!
Shout dat song:
Shake 'em up an' shake 'em up
All night long.
     Hey! Hey!
     Ho . . . Hum!
     Do it, Mr. Charlie,
     Till de red dawn come.

GLORY HALLELUJAH

Judgment Day

They put ma body in the ground,
Ma soul went flyin' o' de town.

Lord Jesus!

Went flyin' to de stars an' moon
A-shoutin', God, I's comin' soon.

O Jesus!

Lord in heaben,
Crown on His head,
Says don't be 'fraid
Cause you ain't dead.

Kind Jesus!

An' now I'm settin' clean an' bright
In de sweet o' ma Lord's sight,—
          Clean an' bright,
                    Clean an' bright.

Prayer Meeting

Glory! Halleluiah!
De dawn's a-comin'!
Glory! Halleluiah!
De dawn's a-comin'!
A black old woman
In the amen-corner of the
Ebecanezer Baptist Church.
A black old woman croons,
De dawn's a-comin'!

.

Feet O' Jesus

At de feet o' Jesus,
Sorrow like a sea.
Lordy, let yo' mercy
Come driftin' down on me.

At de feet o' Jesus,
At yo' feet I stand.
O, ma little Jesus,
Please reach out yo' hand.

Prayer

I ask you this:
Which way to go?
I ask you this:
Which sin to bear?
Which crown to put
Upon my hair?
I do not know,
Lord God,
I do not know.

Shout

Listen to yo' prophets,
        Little Jesus!
Listen to yo' saints!

Fire

Fire,
Fire, Lord!
Fire gonna burn ma soul!

I ain't been good,
I ain't been clean,—
I been stinkin', low-down, mean.

Fire,
Fire, Lord!
Fire gonna burn ma soul!

Tell me, brother,
Do you believe
If you wanta go to heaben
Got to moan an' grieve?

Fire,
Fire, Lord!
Fire gonna burn ma soul!

I been stealin',
Been tellin' lies,
Had more women
Than Pharaoh had wives.

Fire,
Fire, Lord!
Fire gonna burn ma soul!
I means Fire, Lord!
Fire gonna burn ma soul!

Moan

I'm deep in trouble,
Nobody to understand,
      Lord, Lord!

Deep in trouble,
Nobody to understand,
      O, Lord!

Gonna pray to ma Jesus,
Ask him to gimme His hand.
      Ma Lord!

I'm moanin', moanin',
Nobody cares just why.
      No, Lord!

Moanin', moanin',
Feels like I could die.
      O, Lord!

Sho, there must be peace,
      Ma Jesus,
Somewhere in yo' sky.
      Yes, Lord!

Angels Wings

De angels wings is white as snow,
        O, white as snow,
                White
                            as
                                    snow.
De angels wings is white as snow,
        But I drug ma wings
        In de dirty mire.
        O, I drug ma wings
        All through the fire.
But de angels wings is white as snow,
        White
                as
                    snow.

.

Sinner

Have mercy, Lord!

Po' an' black
An' humble an' lonesome
An' a sinner in yo' sight.

Have mercy, Lord!

Beale Street Love

Beale Street Love

Love
Is a brown man's fist
With hard knuckles
Crushing the lips,
Blackening the eyes,—
Hit me again,
Says Clorinda.

Cora

I broke ma heart this mornin'.
Ain't got no heart no mo'.
Next time a man comes near me
Gonna shut an' lock ma door
Cause they treat me mean,—
The ones I loves.
They always treat me mean.

Workin' Man

I works all day
Wid a pick an' a shovel.
Comes home at night,—
It ain't nothin' but a hovel.

I calls for ma woman
When I opens de door.
She's out in de street,—
Ain't nothin' but a 'hore.

I does her good
An' I treats her fine,
But she don't gimme lovin'
Cause she ain't de right kind.

I'm a hard workin' man
An' I sho pays double
Cause I tries to be good
An' gits nothin' but trouble.

Bad Luck Card

Cause you don't love me
Is awful, awful hard.
Gypsy done showed me
Ma bad luck card.

There ain't no good left
In this world for me.
Gypsy done tole me,—
Unlucky as can be.

I don't know what
Po' weary me can do.
Gypsy says I'd kill ma self
If I was you.

Baby

Albert!
Hey, Albert!
Don't you play in dat road.
        You see dem trucks
        A goin' by.
        One run ovah you
        An' you die.
Albert, don't you play in dat road.

Evil Woman

I ain't gonna mistreat ma
Good gal any more.
I'm just gonna kill her
Next time she makes me sore.

I treats her kind but
She don't do me right.
She fights an' quarrels most
Ever night.

I can't have no woman's
Got such low-down ways,
Cause a blue-gummed woman
Ain't de style now days.

I brought her from de South
An' she's goin' on back
Else I'll use her head
For a carpet tack.

A Ruined Gal

Standin' by de lonesome riverside
After de boat's done gone,
     Po' weary me
     Won't be nobody's bride
     Cause I is long gone wrong.

Standin' by de weary riverside
When de boat comes in,
     Po' lonesome me
     Won't meet nobody
     Cause I ain't got no friend.

By de edge o' de weary riverside
Night-time's comin' down.
     Ain't nothin' for a ruined gal
     But jump overboard an' drown.

O, de lonesome riverside,
O, de wicked water.
     Damn ma black old mammy's soul
     For ever havin' a daughter.

Minnie Sings Her Blues

Cabaret, cabaret!
That's where ma man an' me go.
Cabaret, cabaret!
That's where we go,—
Leaves de snow outside
An' our troubles at de door.

Jazz band, jazz band!
Ma man an' me dance.
When I cuddles up to him
No other gal's got a chance.

Baby, O, Baby,
I'm midnight mad.
If ma daddy didn't love me
It sho would be sad.
If he didn't love me
I'd go away
An' dig me a grave this very day.

Blues . . . blues!
Blue, blue, blues!
I'd sho have them blues.

Dressed Up

I had ma clothes cleaned
Just like new.
I put 'em on but
I still feels blue.

I bought a new hat,
Sho is fine,
But I wish I had back that
Old gal o' mine.

I got new shoes,—
They don't hurt ma feet,
But I ain't got nobody
For to call me sweet.

Black Gal

I's always been a workin' girl.
I treated Albert fine.
Ain't cut him wid no razor,
Ain't never been unkind.

Yet it seems like always
Men takes all they can from me
Then they goes an' finds a yaller gal
An' lets me be.

I dressed up Albert Johnson.
I bought him suits o' clothes,
An' soon as he got out de barrel
Then out ma door he goes.

Yet I ain't never been no bad one.
Can't help it cause I'm black.
I hates them rinney yaller gals
An' I wants ma Albert back.
Ma little, short, sweet, brownskin boy,—
Oh, God, I wants him back!

From the
Georgia Roads

Sun Song

Sun and softness,
Sun and the beaten hardness of the earth,
Sun and the song of all the sun-stars
Gathered together,—
Dark ones of Africa,
I bring you my songs
To sing on the Georgia roads.

Magnolia Flowers

The quiet fading out of life
In a corner full of ugliness.

I went lookin' for magnolia flowers
But I didn't find 'em.
I went lookin' for magnolia flowers in the dusk
And there was only this corner
Full of ugliness.

    'Scuse me,
      I didn't mean to stump ma toe on you, lady.

There ought to be magnolias
Somewhere in this dusk.

    'Scuse me,
      I didn't mean to stump ma toe on you.

Mulatto

I am your son, white man!

Georgia dusk
And the turpentine woods.
One of the pillars of the temple fell.

You are my son!
Like hell!

The moon over the turpentine woods.
The Southern night
Full of stars,
Great big yellow stars.
                    Juicy bodies
                    Of nigger wenches
                    Blue black
                    Against black fences.
                    O, you little bastard boy,
                    What's a body but a toy?
The scent of pine wood stings the soft night air.
        What's the body of your mother?
Silver moonlight everywhere.
        What's the body of your mother?
Sharp pine scent in the evening air.
                    A nigger night,
                    A nigger joy,
                    A little yellow
                    Bastard boy.

Naw, you ain't by brother.
Niggers ain't my brother.
Not ever.
Niggers ain't my brother.

The Southern night is full of stars,
Great big yellow stars.
> O, sweet as earth,
> Dusk dark bodies
> Give sweet birth
To little yellow bastard boys.

78

Git on back there in the night,
You ain't white.

The bright stars scatter everywhere.
Pine wood scent in the evening air.
> A nigger night,
> A nigger joy.

I am your son, white man!

> A little yellow
> Bastard boy.

Red Silk Stockings

Put on yo' red silk stockings,
Black gal.
Go out an' let de white boys
Look at yo' legs.

Ain't nothin' to do for you, nohow,
Round this town,—
You's too pretty.
Put on yo' red silk stockings, gal,
An' tomorrow's chile'll
Be a high yaller.

Go out an' let de white boys
Look at yo' legs.

Jazz Band in a Parisian Cabaret

Play that thing,
Jazz band!
Play it for the lords and ladies,
For the dukes and counts,
For the whores and gigolos,
For the American millionaires,
And the school teachers
Out for a spree.
Play it,
Jazz band!
You know that tune
That laughs and cries at the same time.
You know it.

      May I?
      Mais oui.
      Mein Gott!
      Parece una rumba.

Play it, jazz band!
You've got seven languages to speak in
And then some,
Even if you do come from Georgia.

      Can I go home wid yuh, sweetie?
      Sure.

Song for a Dark Girl

Way Down South in Dixie
     (Break the heart of me)
They hung my black young lover
     To a cross roads tree.

Way Down South in Dixie
     (Bruised body high in air)
I asked the white Lord Jesus
     What was the use of prayer.

Way Down South in Dixie
     (Break the heart of me)
Love is a naked shadow
     On a gnarled and naked tree.

Mammy

I'm waiting for ma mammy,—
    She is Death.

Say it very softly.
Say it very slowly if you choose.

I'm waiting for ma mammy,—
    Death.

.

Laughers

Dream singers,
Story tellers,
Dancers,
Loud laughers in the hands of Fate—
        My people.
Dish-washers,
Elevator-boys,
Ladies' maids,
Crap-shooters,
Cooks,
Waiters,
Jazzers,
Nurses of babies,
Loaders of ships,
Rounders,
Number writers,
Comedians in vaudeville
And band-men in circuses—
Dream-singers all,—
        My people.
Story-tellers all,—
        My people.
        Dancers—
God! What dancers!
        Singers—
God! What singers!
Singers and dancers.
Dancers and laughers.
        Laughers?
Yes, laughers…laughers…laughers—
Loud-mouthed laughers in the hands
        Of Fate.

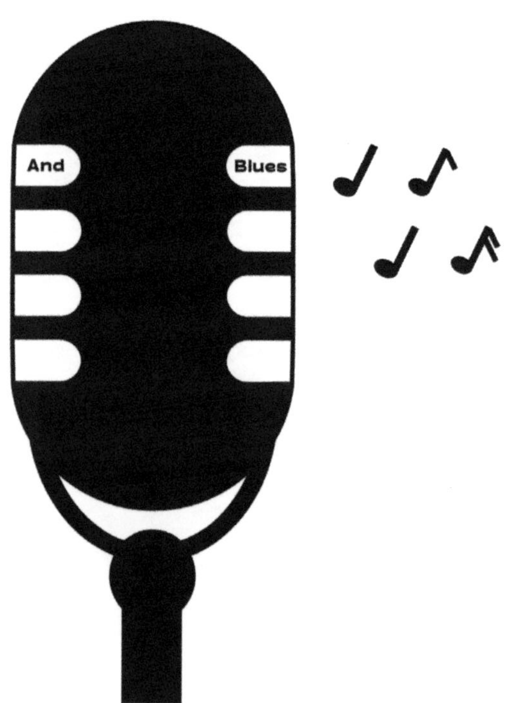
And
Blues

Lament Over Love

I hope ma chile'll
Never love a man.
I say I hope ma chile'll
Never love a man.
Cause love can hurt you
Mo'n anything else can.

I'm goin' down to de river
An' I ain't goin' there to swim.
Goin' down to de river,
Ain't goin' there to swim.
Ma true love's left me, an'
I'm goin' there to think about him.

Love is like whiskey,
Love is like red, red wine.
Love is like whiskey,
O, like sweet red wine.
If you want to be happy
You got to love all de time.

I'm goin' up in a tower
Tall as a tree is tall,
Say up in a tower
Tall as a tree is tall.
Gonna think about ma man an'
Let ma fool-self fall.

Gal's Cry for a Dying Lover

Heard de owl a hootin',
Knowed somebody's 'bout to die.
Heard de owl a hootin',
Knowed somebody's 'bout to die.
Put ma head un'neath de kiver,
Started in to moan an' cry.

Hound dawg's barkin'
Mean's he's gonna leave this world.
Hound dawg's barkin'
Mean's he's gonna leave this world.
O, Lawd have mercy
On a po' black girl.

Black an' ugly
But he sho do treat me kind.
I'm black an' ugly
But he sho do treat me kind.
High-in-heaben Jesus,
Please don't take this man o' mine.

Young Gal's Blues

I'm gonna walk to de graveyard
'Hind ma friend Miss Cora Lee.
Gonna walk to de graveyard
'Hind ma dear friend Cora Lee
Cause when I'm dead some
Body'll have to walk behind me.

I'm goin' to de po' house
To see ma old Aunt Clew.
Goin' to de po' house
To see ma old Aunt Clew.
When I'm old an' ugly
I'll want to see somebody, too.

De po' house is lonely
An' de grave is cold.
O, de po' house is lonely,
De graveyard grave is cold.
But I'd rather be dead than
To be ugly an' old.

When love is gone what
Can a young gal do?
When love is gone, O,
What can a young gal do?
Keep on a-lovin' me, daddy,
Cause I don't want to be blue.

Midwinter Blues

In de middle of de winter,
Snow all over de ground.
In de middle of de winter,
Snow all over de ground,—
'Twas de night befo' Christmas
Ma good man turned me down.

Don' know's I'd mind his goin'
But he left me when de coal was low.
Don' know's I'd mind his goin'
But he left when de coal was low.
Now, if a man loves a woman
That ain't no time to go.

He told me that he loved me
But he must a been tellin' a lie.
He told me that he loved me.
He must a been tellin' a lie.
But he's the only man I'll
Love till de day I die.

I'm gonna buy me a rose bud
An' plant it at ma back door,
Buy me a rose bud,
Plant it at ma back door,
So when I'm dead they
Won't need no flowers from de store.

Listen Here Blues

Sweet girls, sweet girls,
Listen here to me.
All you sweet girls,
Listen here to me:
Gin an' whiskey
Kin make you lose yo' 'ginity.

I used to be a good chile,
Lawd, in Sunday School.
Used to be a good chile,—
Always in Sunday School,
Till these licker-headed rounders
Made me everbody's fool.

Good girls, good girls,
Listen here to me.
Oh, you good girls,
Better listen to me:
Don't you fool wid no men cause
They'll bring you misery.

Hard Daddy

I went to ma daddy,
Says Daddy I have got de blues.
Went to ma daddy,
Says Daddy I have got de blues.
Ma daddy says Honey
Can't you bring no better news?

I cried on his shoulder but
He turned his back on me.
Cried on his shoulder but
He turned his back on me.
He said a woman's cryin's
Never gonna bother me.

I wish I had wings to
Fly like de eagle flies.
Wish I had wings to
Fly like de eagle flies.
I'd fly on ma man an'
I'd scratch out both his eyes.

Bound No'th Blues

Goin' down de road, Lawd,
Goin' down de road.
Down de road, Lawd,
Way, way down de road.
Got to find somebody
To help me carry dis load.

Road's in front o' me,
Nothin' to do but walk.
Road's in front o' me,
Walk…and walk…and walk.
I'd like to meet a good friend
To come along an' talk.

Hates to be lonely,
Lawd, I hates to be sad.
Says I hates to be lonely,
Hates to be lonely an' sad,
But ever friend you finds seems
Like they try to do you bad.

Road, road, road, O!
Road, road…road…road, road!
Road, road, road, O!
On de No'thern road.
These Mississippi towns ain't
Fit fer a hoppin' toad.

Ma Man

When ma man looks at me
He knocks me off ma feet.
When ma man looks at me
He knocks me off ma feet.
He's got those 'lectric-shockin' eyes an'
De way he shocks me sho is sweet.

He kin play a banjo.
Lordy, he kin plunk, plunk, plunk.
He kin play a banjo.
I mean plunk, plunk . . . plunk, plunk.
He plays good when he's sober
An' better, better, better when he's drunk.

Eagle-rockin',
Daddy, eagle-rock with me.
Eagle rockin',
Come an' eagle-rock with me.
Honey baby,
Eagle-rockish as I kin be!

Hey! Hey!

Sun's a risin',
This is gonna be ma song.
Sun's a risin',
This is gonna be ma song.
I could be blue but
I been blue all night long.